☑ W9-BQZ-214

THE HUMAN MACHINE

THE
PRODUCTION LINE

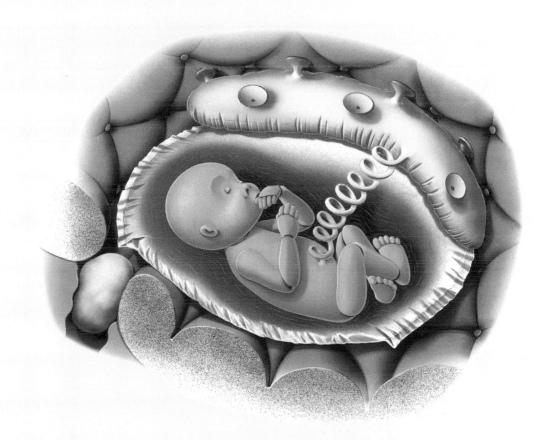

Sarah Angliss

Illustrations by Tom Connell

Thameside Press

U.S. publication copyright © 1999 Thameside Press.
International copyright reserved in all countries.
No part of this book may be reproduced in any
form without written permission from the publisher.

Distributed in the United States by
Smart Apple Media
123 South Broad Street
Mankato, Minnesota 56001

Text copyright © Sarah Angliss 1999

Editor: Susie Brooks
Designer: Helen James
Educational consultant: Carol Ballard

Printed in Singapore

ISBN 1-929298-20-X
Library of Congress Catalog Card Number 99-73411

10 9 8 7 6 5 4 3 2 1

Words in **bold** are explained in the glossary on pages 30 and 31.

CONTENTS

THE PRODUCTION LINE

Think of your body as an amazing machine—a human machine. Its many parts were all formed on a special production line. Your parents gave you life by creating a single cell, no bigger than a speck of dust. This cell developed inside your mother until it became a baby.

Making babies

As you grow into an adult, you'll develop all the body parts you need to become a parent yourself. These parts make up your **reproductive system**.

Men and women have different reproductive systems. A new human can only be created when ingredients from a woman and a man are brought together. Making a new life in this way is called **reproduction**.

Changing shape

By the time you were born you had already spent time on the production line. Inside your mother's body, the cell you started out as divided, again and again, forming millions of new ones. You were born when these cells became a fully formed baby. Then you developed into a child. Your body will continue to grow and change until you are an adult.

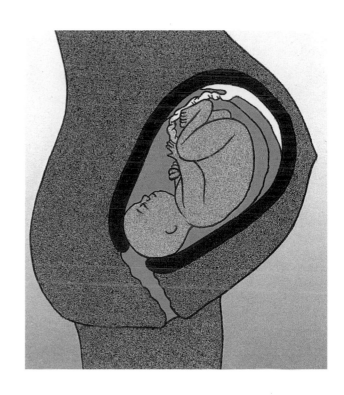

That's not me!

We know that you don't look like the figures in this circle! The main pictures in this book are drawn with a bit of imagination. But look at each one carefully—they show how parts of your reproductive system develop and work. Diagrams like the one above show what some parts really look like—and where in your body they are found.

Breakdown!

Just like any other machine, the human machine needs plenty of care and attention. Sometimes it can go wrong so we need to give it a helping hand. Tool boxes like this one show you some of the problems that can occur in reproduction and growing up.

ONE MAKE— TWO MODELS

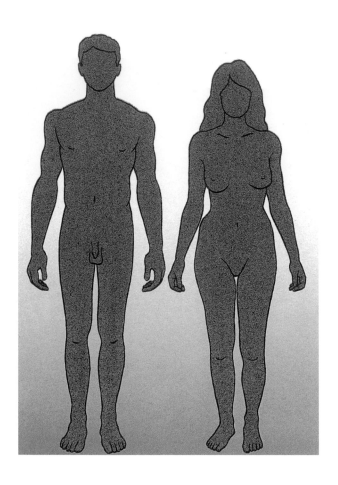

Girls and boys are like two versions of the same machine. They have some very important differences. When they develop as teenagers, these differences increase.

hair grows in new places

breasts develop and hips widen

Changing shape

Until you're about ten years old, you simply get bigger and taller as you grow. But when you reach this age, you begin to show signs of some huge changes. These make the differences between growing boys and girls greater than ever before. They transform you into men and women who are able to reproduce—make babies.

The changes take three or four years to happen. During that time—called **adolescence**—boys develop stronger muscles and girls grow larger breasts and hips. A boy's **penis** and **scrotum** enlarge, and his voice becomes deeper. Both girls and boys make more sweat and grow hair in new places.

6

Liking each other

When we reach adolescence, most of us develop a new interest—curiosity in the opposite sex. Our interest in each other has an important purpose, as well as being enormous fun. Men and women need to be together if they want to make babies. We usually find out how much we like each other as we develop into adults.

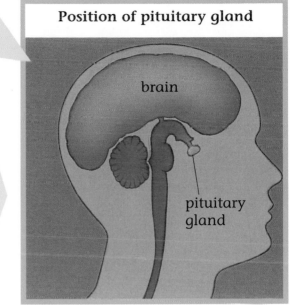

Position of pituitary gland

brain

pituitary gland

voice deepens

Signal box

The time that these body changes start is called **puberty**. A tiny organ at the base of the brain, called the **pituitary gland**, acts like an emergency control center while they are taking place. It produces chemicals, called **hormones**, that are sent around the body, telling important parts how to develop.

hair grows in new places

The changes you see on the outside during puberty are only a tiny part of the story. To find out what happens on the inside, see pages 8-11.

penis and scrotum grow larger

Side effects

Our bodies go through so many changes during adolescence, it's no wonder we suffer a few side effects. Many of us have to put up with moody spells and spots as teenagers. These are often caused by the rush of hormones that tell our bodies how to change. Fortunately, such problems don't last forever —once adolescence is over, they usually fade away.

SPERM SUPPLY

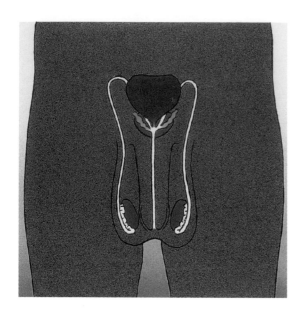

boy has a pair of organs, called testes, that set to work like factories as he develops into a man. They begin to produce sperm—one of the two ingredients needed to make a baby. The boy's penis acts as a delivery pipe for these sperm.

glands make juices for semen

Cold stores

The **testes** are a man's **sperm** factories. They also make a **hormone** that manages their work, telling them how many sperm to produce. The testes are packed with narrow coiled tubes, stored in a pouch called the **scrotum**. This dangles outside the man's body, keeping the sperm cool.

Ready for action

When sperm are in storage, they lie still. But as soon as a man's sperm delivery system goes into action, their tails start moving to and fro like flippers, pushing them forward.

Glands around the base of the **penis** make juices that help the sperm to move. These mix to form a liquid called **semen**. Most boys start making semen when they reach **puberty**.

Even when he is a baby, a boy uses his penis to let **urine** out of his body. But after puberty, his penis becomes an important part of his **reproductive system**, acting as a delivery pipe for sperm and semen too.

What sets sperm into action? Where do they go? Find out on pages 12-15.

Battery pack

Semen is more than just a runny fluid that the sperm can swim in. It's also their liquid fuel supply. Semen contains chemicals, called **nutrients**, that can be broken down by sperm to release energy. Sperm need lots of energy as they have to survive a long journey through the penis and beyond.

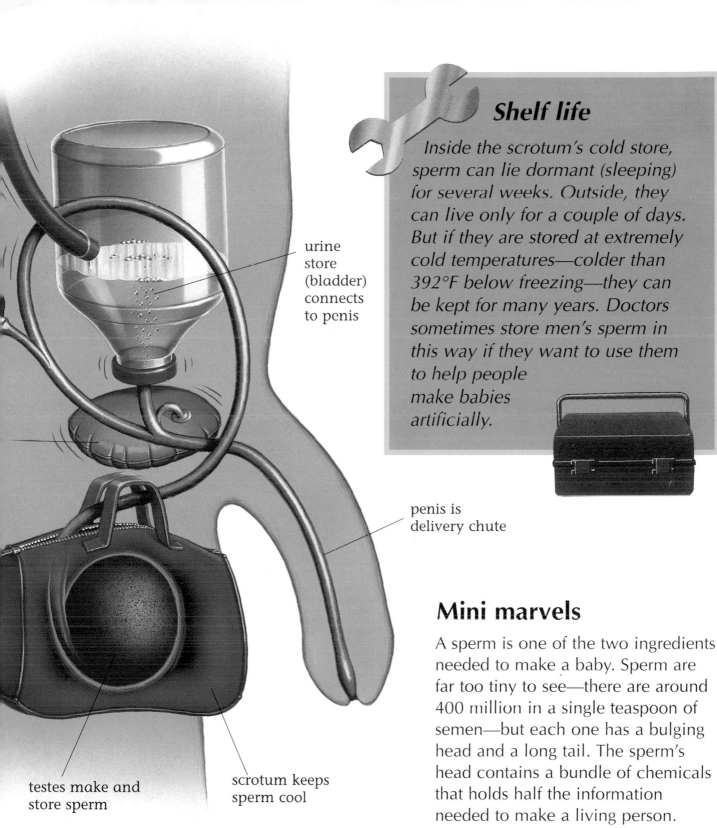

urine store (bladder) connects to penis

penis is delivery chute

testes make and store sperm

scrotum keeps sperm cool

Shelf life

Inside the scrotum's cold store, sperm can lie dormant (sleeping) for several weeks. Outside, they can live only for a couple of days. But if they are stored at extremely cold temperatures—colder than 392°F below freezing—they can be kept for many years. Doctors sometimes store men's sperm in this way if they want to use them to help people make babies artificially.

Mini marvels

A sperm is one of the two ingredients needed to make a baby. Sperm are far too tiny to see—there are around 400 million in a single teaspoon of semen—but each one has a bulging head and a long tail. The sperm's head contains a bundle of chemicals that holds half the information needed to make a living person.

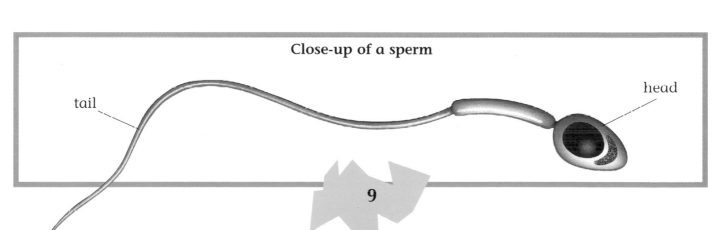

Close-up of a sperm

tail

head

9

EGG FACTORY

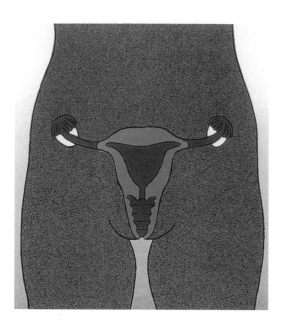

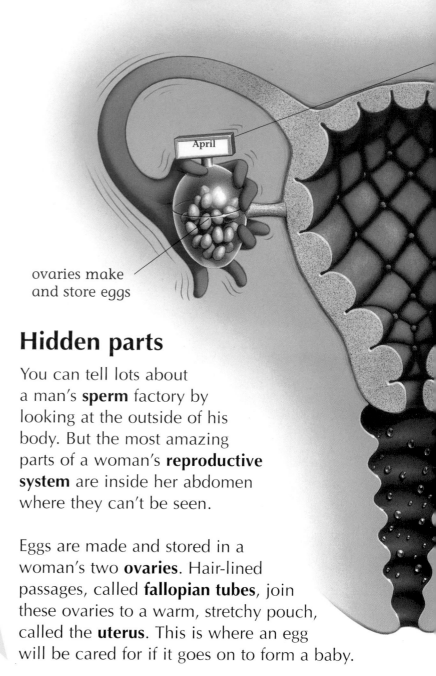

ovaries make
and store eggs

Even before she is born, a girl has a store of tiny eggs. As she becomes a woman, her body turns on a timer that makes her release one of these eggs every month.

Life supply

A woman's ovaries contain many more eggs than she'll ever need. When a girl is born, she will already have between 400 000 and 800 000 eggs in store. But fewer than 500 of these are likely to be released during her lifetime—and only the tiniest fraction may be given the chance to create a new human life.

Hidden parts

You can tell lots about a man's **sperm** factory by looking at the outside of his body. But the most amazing parts of a woman's **reproductive system** are inside her abdomen where they can't be seen.

Eggs are made and stored in a woman's two **ovaries**. Hair-lined passages, called **fallopian tubes**, join these ovaries to a warm, stretchy pouch, called the **uterus**. This is where an egg will be cared for if it goes on to form a baby.

Tiny treasures

Unlike a hen's eggs, a woman's eggs are no bigger than specks of dust. Rather than hard shells, they have a soft coating. Just like sperm, each one of them contains a bundle of chemicals that hold half the instructions needed to make a human.

An egg and sperm can go on to form a baby only if they join together.

ovaries take it in turns to release monthly egg

How do a sperm and egg join together? Find out on pages 12-15.

fallopian tubes link ovaries to uterus

May

uterus has thick lining

vagina is stretchy tube

In balance

*Many **hormones** are working all the time to keep a woman's egg supply going. These may make her feel uncomfortable, tired or upset a day or so before her period. Rest, a good diet, and some gentle exercise can all help to keep these feelings away.*

Monthly delivery

About once a month, an egg moves out of one ovary and into a fallopian tube. Hairs in the tube beat to waft the egg along it. As this happens, the tube ripples in a special rhythm to help the egg move. The next month, the opposite ovary will send an egg along.

If an egg meets a sperm in the fallopian tube, it may move to the uterus to develop into a baby. Otherwise it dies after a couple of days and the woman's body sheds it, along with the lining of her uterus, through a tube called her **vagina**. The time every month when this happens is often called a **period**. After the lining is shed, a new one grows and gradually thickens, ready for the next egg.

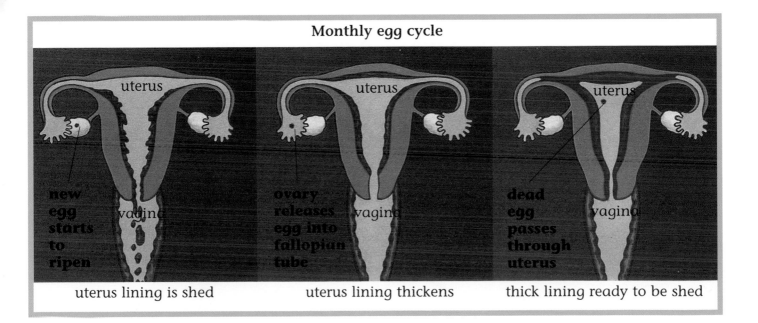

Monthly egg cycle

uterus	uterus	uterus
new egg starts to ripen — vagina	ovary releases egg into fallopian tube — vagina	dead egg passes through uterus — vagina
uterus lining is shed	uterus lining thickens	thick lining ready to be shed

PERFECT FIT

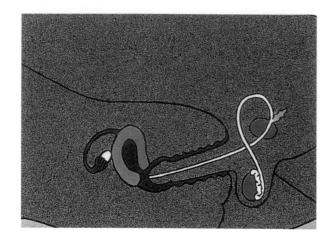

Men and women are perfectly designed to fit together. Joining can make them feel wonderful. It can also enable them to bring together a sperm and egg—the two ingredients that make a baby.

Close comfort

If a man and woman love each other very much, they may like to cuddle up so closely, their bodies join. Getting together in this way is called **sexual intercourse**, making love, having sex, or simply sex.

Getting together

When people feel aroused (in the mood for sex) chemical signals, called **hormones**, make their bodies change so it's easier for them to join. These hormones are made and sent out by the brain's **pituitary gland**.

Among other changes, this rush of hormones makes the couple's hearts beat faster, pumping more blood into their sexual parts. Like air in a tire, the extra blood inflates these body parts. The man's **penis** becomes firmer, enabling it to slide inside the woman's **vagina**.

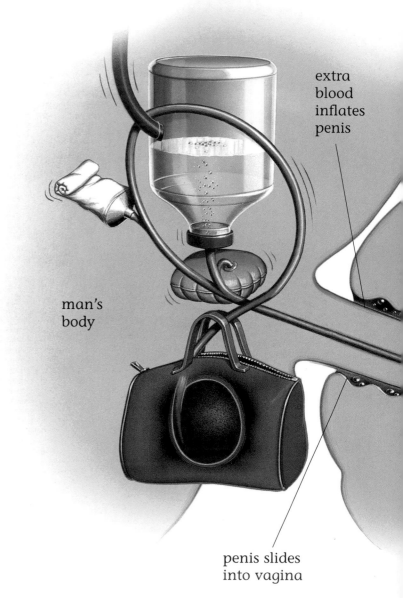

extra blood inflates penis

man's body

penis slides into vagina

Special touch

Even when they are very young, many people like to touch and play with their own sexual parts. This gives them enjoyable feelings, very like the ones they may have as adults when they have sex. This activity is called **masturbation**. It's a good way for people to find out which parts of their own body give them pleasure.

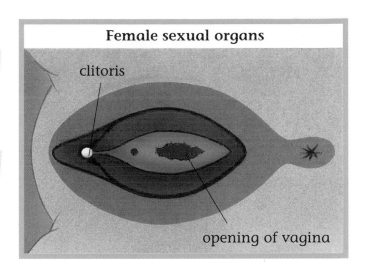

Female sexual organs

clitoris

opening of vagina

Sensational stuff

Glands at the top of the woman's vagina make slippery juices that oil it, so the man's penis can move in and out of her easily. A penis is very sensitive to touch —so is a woman's vagina and the delicate mound in front of it, called the **clitoris**.

A couple may move together during sex, to enjoy the feelings these parts produce. When they do this, the enjoyable feelings they experience often become stronger. Eventually they may reach a peak, called an **orgasm**, which makes ripples of pleasure travel through their bodies.

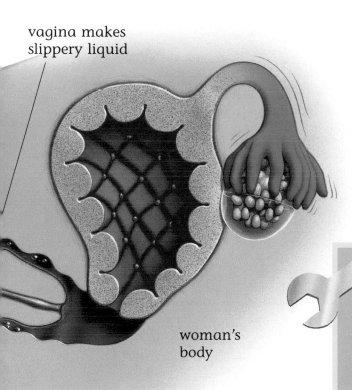

vagina makes slippery liquid

woman's body

How else does the pituitary gland change our bodies? Find out on pages 6-7.

In the mind

Sex may be something that people do with their bodies, but it actually begins in the mind. People usually enjoy having sex because they like the look, smell, touch or even the sound of their partner. But if a person doesn't feel comfortable or safe with someone else, they are unlikely to become aroused.

MODEL MAKING

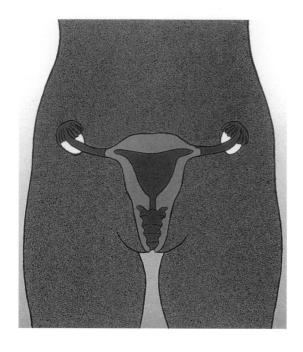

Sexual intercourse gives a man and woman the chance to make a sperm meet an egg. Millions of sperm can be delivered into a woman's body during sex. But only one of them will be able to join any waiting egg.

Jet-set journey

When a man has an **orgasm**, about a teaspoon of **semen**, enriched with around 400 million **sperm**, pumps out of his **penis** and into the top of the woman's **vagina**. This is called **ejaculation**.

Fuelled by the semen, the sperm move through a tiny ring-shaped opening, called the **cervix**, into the woman's **uterus**. Then they swim towards her **fallopian tubes**. The uterus walls ripple when a woman has an orgasm, helping the sperm along.

Journey of sperm to egg

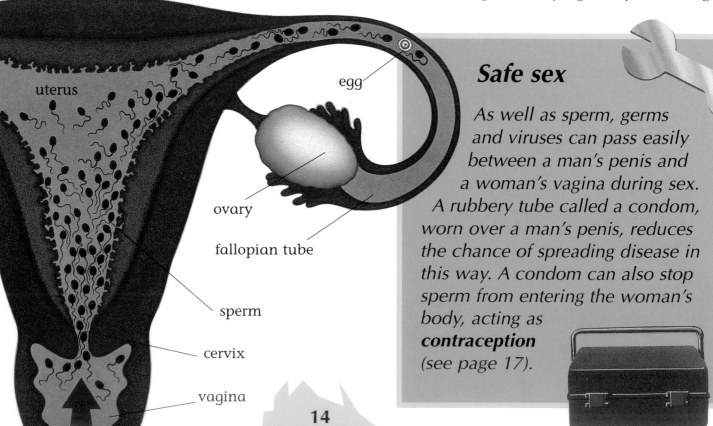

uterus

egg

ovary

fallopian tube

sperm

cervix

vagina

Safe sex

As well as sperm, germs and viruses can pass easily between a man's penis and a woman's vagina during sex. A rubbery tube called a condom, worn over a man's penis, reduces the chance of spreading disease in this way. A condom can also stop sperm from entering the woman's body, acting as ***contraception*** *(see page 17).*

14

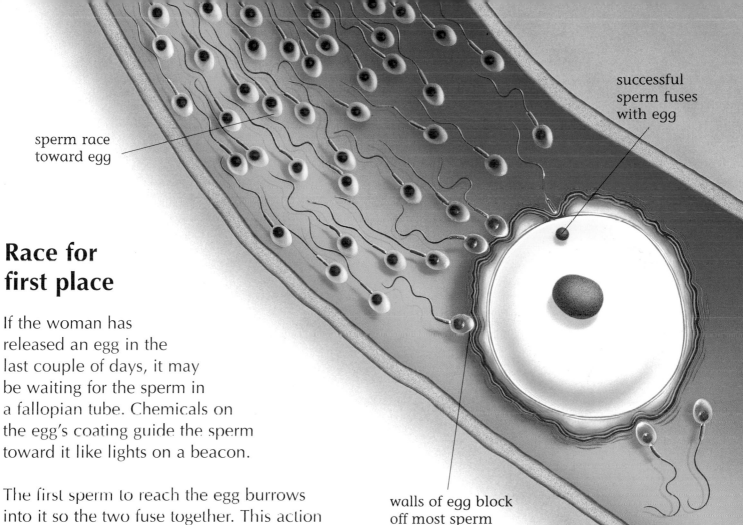

sperm race
toward egg

successful
sperm fuses
with egg

walls of egg block
off most sperm

Race for first place

If the woman has released an egg in the last couple of days, it may be waiting for the sperm in a fallopian tube. Chemicals on the egg's coating guide the sperm toward it like lights on a beacon.

The first sperm to reach the egg burrows into it so the two fuse together. This action is called **fertilization**. As soon as it happens, the egg's coating hardens, blocking off other sperm like a brick wall and creating a new **cell** called a **zygote**. This is the moment of **conception**. It means a new life can begin.

Survival time

It takes about an hour for sperm to travel just a few inches from the cervix to the fallopian tubes. But sperm can survive for up to two days inside a woman's body, so it's possible for a woman to conceive two days after having sex. Sperm can leak into a woman's body, enabling her to conceive, even if the man she is having sex with does not ejaculate.

Personal formula

Every new human is made up of billions of cells—individual building blocks that make up every body part. The zygote is the first one of these.

Chemical instructions inside the zygote tell it how to divide, many times over, until it forms a baby that is ready to enter the world. These instructions are called **genes**.

Half of your genes come from your mother's egg, and half are from your father's sperm. That's why you may be like your parents in some ways.

TAKING SHAPE

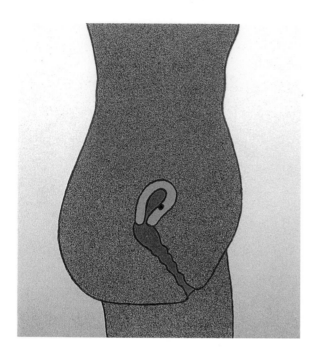

Many ordinary machines are made by putting parts together or pouring them into molds. But a human finds its own shape. Built-in instructions tell a zygote how to divide over and over again to form a person.

ball of cells
roots itself in
uterus lining

Life's lottery

*The human production line doesn't always work as you'd expect. When an egg meets a **sperm**, there's a one in ten chance that it won't be fertilized. If **fertilization** does occur, there's a one in three chance that the zygote won't root itself in the uterus, and a six in ten chance that it will die within a week. In all, fewer than three in ten eggs that meet a sperm go on to become babies.*

Splitting cells

As soon as a **zygote** forms, hairs inside the **fallopian tube** begin to waft it toward the **uterus**. This journey takes about three days. In that time the zygote divides to form a ball of two, four, eight, then sixteen **cells**.

Within a week, the ball of cells drops into the uterus. Here it can root itself in the thick lining, making the woman **pregnant**. Safely cushioned and nourished by the lining of the uterus, the ball of cells continues to divide.

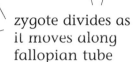

zygote divides as
it moves along
fallopian tube

Production prevention

Many people want to enjoy having sex without making a baby. That's why they use **contraception**—something that stops a sperm meeting an egg. There are many forms of contraception. Most of them reduce the chance of conception, but none can guarantee to prevent it altogether. The only way to be sure of this is to have no sex at all.

Shaping up

Four weeks after **conception**, the zygote has turned into a group of cells that's still smaller than your little fingernail. Although it's tiny, it already shows traces of human form.

At this stage, the developing baby is called an **embryo**. It has four tiny buds that will grow into legs and arms. It also has the beginnings of its eyes, mouth, spine, and brain.

Looking life-like

Within ten weeks, the embryo has grown to about the length of your little finger. It weighs no more than a teaspoon of sugar, but it already looks like either a boy or a girl.

Now it is called a **fetus**. Its arms and legs have grown, its brain has developed further, and its eyes and ears have fully formed. So has its heart, which has begun to beat.

The developing embryo

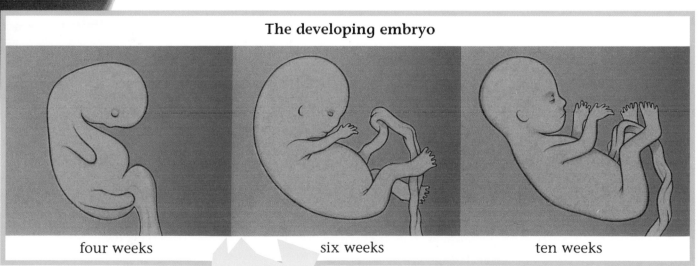

| four weeks | six weeks | ten weeks |

BABY BAG

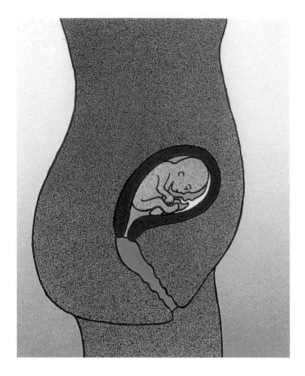

A growing embryo needs food, warmth, and energy. It also needs a supply of oxygen and a way to get rid of waste. The uterus is a stretchy bag that protects and feeds the baby as it develops.

Special service

An **embryo** is unable to eat or breathe on its own. It relies on its mother for food and **oxygen**. A woman's **uterus** can give her embryo all the care, protection, and **nutrients** it needs to develop.

If all goes well, a baby will spend nine months growing inside this bag. By the time it's ready to be born, it should be around 14 inches long and as heavy as three or four bags of sugar.

Soft sack

Inside the uterus, a baby floats in a sack of watery liquid, called **amniotic fluid**. This acts like a shock-absorber, cushioning the baby from bumps and preventing it from being squashed.

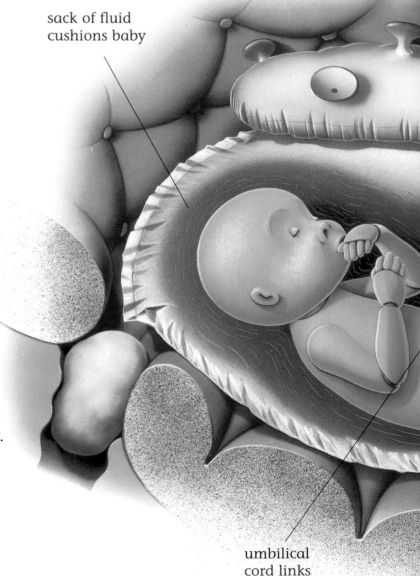

sack of fluid cushions baby

umbilical cord links baby to placenta

What a picture

These days, a woman can see what her baby looks like months before it is born, by having an **ultrasound scan**. An ultrasound machine bounces high-pitched sound waves off the baby and makes them into a moving picture on a screen. This enables doctors to check that the baby is healthy.

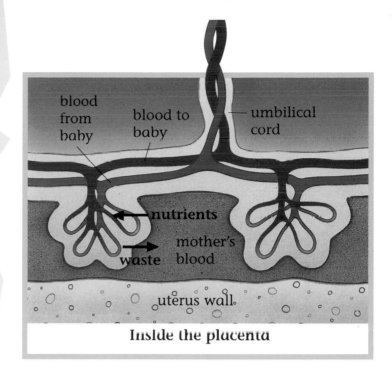

blood from baby

blood to baby

umbilical cord

nutrients

mother's blood

waste

uterus wall

Inside the placenta

placenta is filter for food, waste and poisons

Food filter

Life-giving food and oxygen are delivered to an embryo by its mother's blood. These supplies reach the baby through a thick web of tissue, called the **placenta**. The placenta grows on the uterus wall. It's connected to the embryo by an **umbilical cord**.

The baby's **blood vessels** run through the umbilical cord to the placenta. Here, they come very close to the mother's blood vessels. The placenta acts like a filter. It lets nutrients from the mother's blood pass into the child's blood. At the same time, it lets waste from the baby's blood pass into the mother's blood.

Passing poison

A thin layer of **cells** separates the mother's blood from the baby's inside the placenta. This acts like a barrier, stopping some everyday poisons from reaching the child. Unfortunately some poisons can still force their way through. If a **pregnant** woman smokes, her baby may be harmed by the chemicals in her cigarettes. Too much alcohol can also damage a developing baby for life.

STRETCHY SHELTER

placenta sends signals to breasts, telling them to make milk

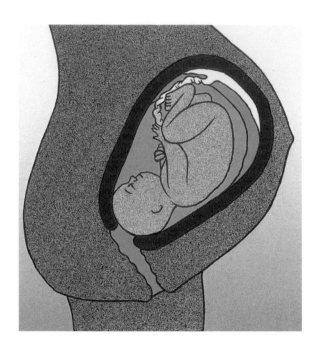

When a woman is pregnant, her body sets up some emergency procedures. These transform her body so it can take care of her developing baby, making room for it while it grows.

All change

A bulge starts to show in a woman's abdomen when she's about 16 weeks **pregnant**. But astounding changes take place in her body from the moment of **conception**. Like all other changes, these are controlled by **hormones**—the body's chemical messengers.

Action stations

As soon as a woman has conceived, new hormones send out emergency messages to many parts of her body. They tell her **ovaries** to stop releasing eggs for a while. They also make her body store more **calcium** —the **nutrient** she will need to make the baby's bones. Hormones also cause a woman's **periods** to stop, by telling her **uterus** not to shed its lining.

Out too soon

About one in every ten babies is **premature**—born too early. Premature babies are mostly smaller than babies who spend a full nine months in the uterus. They usually need to spend some time in a special box, called an **incubator**. This gives them warmth and **oxygen** until they develop enough to survive in the outside world.

Under test

A missed period can be a sign that a woman is pregnant. But a woman can find out if she is expecting a baby within days of conception. That's because traces of the hormones she makes when she is pregnant enter her urine. A chemical that changes color when these hormones are present can be dipped into her urine as a pregnancy test.

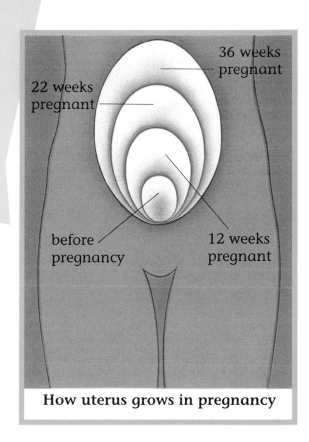

22 weeks pregnant

36 weeks pregnant

before pregnancy

12 weeks pregnant

How uterus grows in pregnancy

growing uterus squashes stomach and other body parts

weight of fetus presses down on bladder

Stretch and squash

Hormones tell a woman's uterus to stretch to make more room for the growing baby. Before she is pregnant, the uterus is smaller than a walnut, but by the time the baby inside her is fully grown, it will probably be bigger than a watermelon.

As it enlarges, the uterus pushes the woman's stomach and many other body parts upward. It also presses down on her **bladder**, the bag that stores her **urine**, so she needs to go to the bathroom more often. Meanwhile, muscles all around the baby become more stretchy, and her **pelvis** gets ready to expand when the baby is born.

Hormones from the woman's **placenta** prepare her breasts to make milk so she can feed the baby after it is born. This makes them grow much larger in size.

DELIVERY DAY

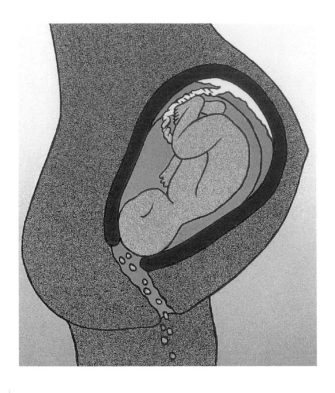

When a baby is ready to be born, the woman needs to squeeze it out of her body, a bit like toothpaste from a tube.

The natural way for a baby to leave its mother's body is through the **vagina**. Squeezing the baby out through this stretchy exit is very hard work —that's probably why the task is called **labor**.

Over and out

A growing **fetus** turns about in the **uterus**, but by the time it's ready to come out it is usually upside down, in order to be born head first.

The mother's **pituitary gland** produces a **hormone** that tells her it's time for the baby to be born. This makes her uterus squeeze on the baby every few seconds, forcing it outward. The first thing that comes out is the **amniotic fluid** that cushioned the baby inside the uterus.

Big squeeze

A newborn baby's skull is made of several separate bony plates that are joined together only loosely. This allows the baby's head to squash slightly as it is squeezed out through the vagina into the world. As a baby grows into a toddler, the bones of its skull become stronger and fuse together, making a tougher box. This is much better at protecting the brain against everyday knocks and bumps.

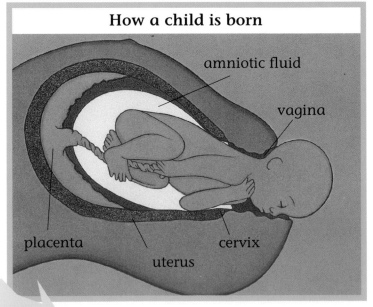

How a child is born

amniotic fluid

vagina

placenta

cervix

uterus

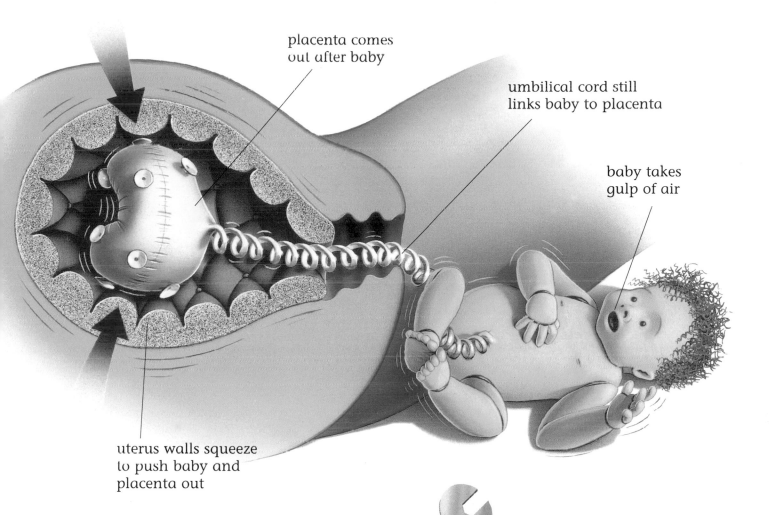

placenta comes out after baby

umbilical cord still links baby to placenta

baby takes gulp of air

uterus walls squeeze to push baby and placenta out

Long labor

As the baby is pushed outward, the **cervix** opens to let the baby's head squeeze through. It can take up to 12 hours just for the head to reach the vagina—and a couple more for the whole body to come out. When the baby has emerged completely, the mother pushes out the **placenta**, which is still joined to the baby by the **umbilical cord**.

On its own

Once the baby is out of its mother, it takes a big gulp of air—a first breath. At this moment, blood starts flowing from its lungs into its heart for the first time. The baby no longer needs the placenta or umbilical cord. Naturally, they'd slowly shrivel up, but medical staff clamp them and cut them away. The remaining stump forms a little scar—the belly button.

Another way

*Sometimes a baby can't leave its mother's body through the vagina. This may be because it is very big, unwell, or in an awkward position. Babies like this can be delivered in an operation called a **Caesarean**. The mother is given a drug that stops her feeling pain and keeps her lower body still. Then her baby is removed through a cut in her abdomen. This operation is usually much shorter than a natural labor.*

BRAND NEW

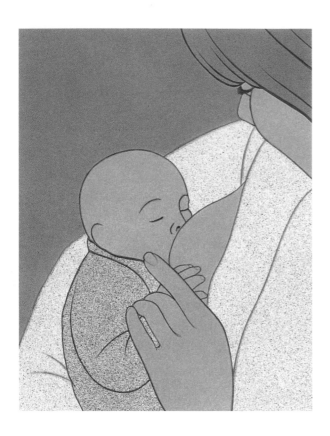

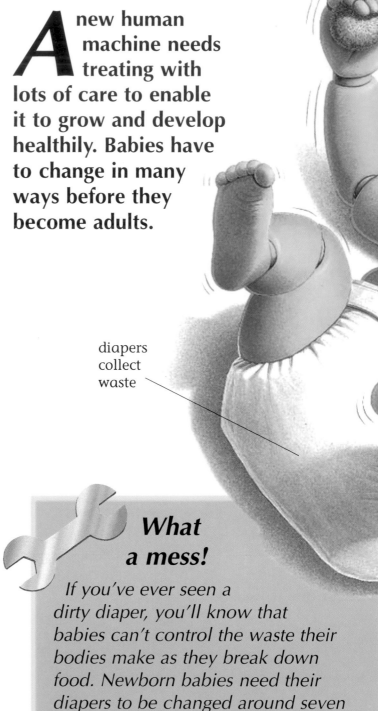

A new human machine needs treating with lots of care to enable it to grow and develop healthily. Babies have to change in many ways before they become adults.

diapers collect waste

Instant reactions

As babies depend on adults to keep them safe, warm, and fed, they need to attract lots of attention. That's why the first thing a baby does is to cry. Another early action is grasping—a new baby has automatic **reflexes** that make it clutch anything that's put into its hand.

Steady progress

It usually takes about three months for a baby just to learn how to lift its own head—and about five more for it to sit upright on its own. By about ten months a baby should be able to crawl—but it could be over a year before it can take a step or say its first word.

What a mess!

If you've ever seen a dirty diaper, you'll know that babies can't control the waste their bodies make as they break down food. Newborn babies need their diapers to be changed around seven times a day. It can take them nearly three years to learn how to use a toilet.

newborn babies have grabbing reflex

new babies may have lots of hair

babies cry to attract attention

Milky marvel

For the first few months of a baby's life, milk is the only food it needs. A **pregnant** woman's **hormones** tell special **cells** in her breasts to start making milk. When a baby sucks on its mother's **nipples**, the mother's brain tells her breasts to produce more of it.

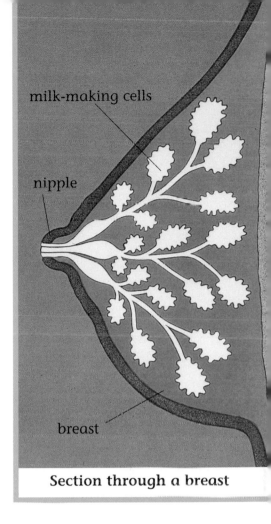

milk-making cells

nipple

breast

Section through a breast

Changing recipe

As well as containing **nutrients**, every mouthful of breast milk also contains special chemicals that can help the baby to fight disease. The ingredients of a mother's milk change gradually to suit her growing baby's needs.

Natural needs

As well as food and warmth, babies also need plenty of love—cuddles, kind words, and other actions that make them feel cared for. As you grow up, you learn how to seek all these important things for yourself. Most people need 18 years —around a fifth of a lifetime—to grow fully and develop their feelings.

Game of life

Games aren't only for fun. Children at play are stretching their imaginations, discovering how the world around them works, and learning how to get along with others. Play helps their minds to develop—and enables them to pick up skills they'll need for life.

CARE AND SERVICING

The human production line is unpredictable. It doesn't always run smoothly, and it can create surprising results. Here are just a few examples.

Out of order

Sometimes parts of a man or woman's **reproductive system** can be blocked or damaged. This makes it difficult for them to conceive. Medical treatment can often help them to produce a baby.

Test-tube treatment

One way of helping a couple start a child is **in vitro fertilization**. A doctor removes ripe eggs from a woman's **ovary** and mixes them with the man's **sperm** in a glass dish or test tube. When one or more of these eggs are fertilized, they are returned to the **uterus** where each one has a chance to implant itself and develop into a baby.

2 eggs are put in glass dish with man's sperm, to be fertilized

3 fertilized egg starts to divide into ball of cells

1 doctor takes eggs from ovary using fine tube

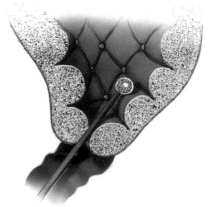

5 ball of cells may implant itself in uterus lining to develop into baby

4 doctor inserts ball of cells into woman's uterus

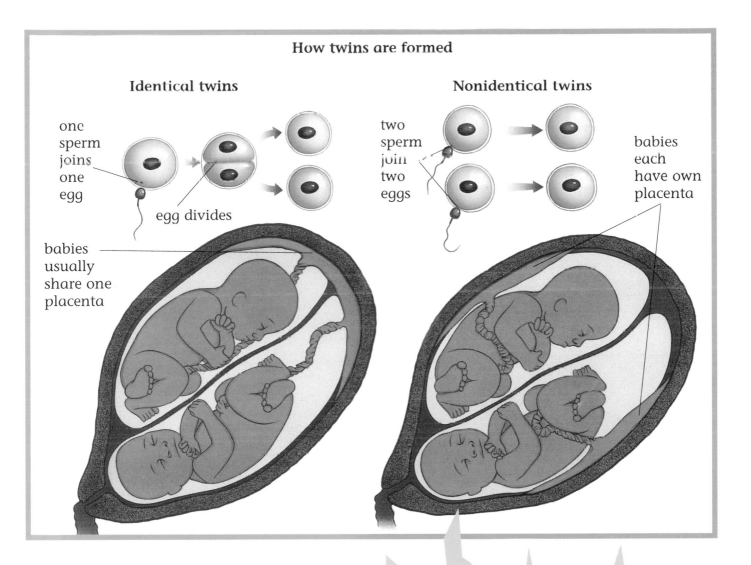

How twins are formed

Identical twins

one sperm joins one egg

egg divides

babies usually share one placenta

Nonidentical twins

two sperm join two eggs

babies each have own placenta

Mass production

Occasionally women produce more than one baby at once—they have a **multiple birth**. In vitro fertilization often leads to the birth of two or more babies.

Two babies born at once are known as twins. There are two types of twin. Identical twins form when a fertilized egg splits into two separate balls of **cells**. The babies that develop are exactly the same. Nonidentical twins form when two different eggs are fertilized at the same time—by two different sperm. These children may be no more alike than ordinary brothers and sisters.

Running repairs

Some parents can pass life-threatening diseases on to their children through their **genes**. The faulty genes may be carried in every cell that divides to create their baby. Doctors already know how to implant a bundle of cells into a uterus to form an **embryo**. If they can find ways to alter the genes that cause diseases before the cells develop, they could give more babies the chance to lead a long, healthy life.

27

OTHER MODELS

Together, a man and woman's reproductive systems have all the equipment they need to make new humans. But some other animals make their young on very different production lines.

Hatching an egg

birds sit on eggs to keep them warm

Shelling out

Not all animals develop in a **uterus**. Birds and reptiles lay eggs, growing their young outside their bodies. An egg that is laid contains a yolk—a special food supply which provides all the **nutrients** the developing **embryo** needs. A hard shell protects the egg on the outside.

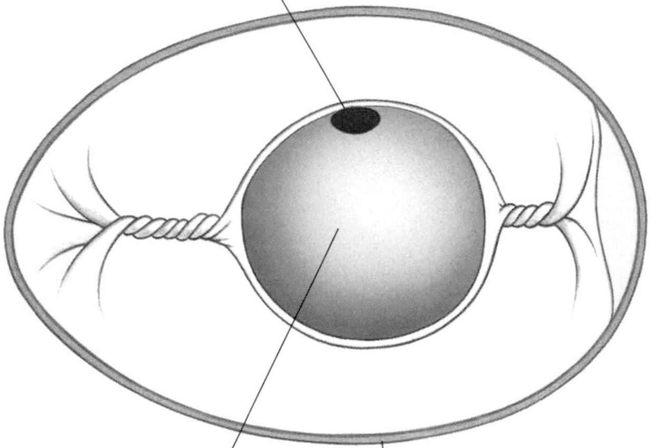

When young are ready to hatch from an egg, they pierce the shell and climb out of it. Newly hatched birds need a lot of looking after, but baby reptiles are like mini-adults—ready to fend for themselves as soon as they are born.

embryo

yolk

shell

babies crack open shell when they're ready to be born

newly-hatched reptiles fend for themselves straight away

kangaroo babies develop in pouch

Body bag

Kangaroos and koalas both come from a group of animals known as **marsupials**. They usually give birth to their young only five weeks after **conception**—before they are fully formed. The newborn young move straight into a pouch on the front of the mother's belly. There they are given warmth and fed with milk until they develop enough to emerge into the outside world.

newborn birds need looking after

Outside option

When humans and many other animals reproduce, the **sperm** meets the egg inside the woman's body. But fish have a different method of **fertilization**. The female fish lays her eggs in water. The male then releases his sperm, which swim through the water to fertilize the eggs.

Carrying time

Different animals carry babies in their uterus for different lengths of time. Dogs are usually **pregnant** for six to eight weeks, while dolphins carry their young for nearly a year. A baby elephant develops inside its mother for as long as 22 months before it is born.

GLOSSARY

adolescence The time when your body becomes like an adult's.

amniotic fluid The watery liquid that completely surrounds a baby in the uterus.

bladder A stretchy sack that stores urine. You empty it when you urinate.

blood vessels The many tubes that carry blood around your body.

Caesarean An operation to deliver a baby through a cut in the mother's abdomen.

calcium The nutrient that makes your bones hard.

cells The billions of very tiny parts that combine to make your body tissues.

cervix The tiny ring-shaped opening at the top of a woman's vagina.

clitoris A sensitive mound of tissue in front of the opening of a woman's vagina.

conception When an egg changes to form a zygote, as an instant result of fertilization.

contraception Reducing the chances of conception during sex, for instance by using a condom or taking hormonal drugs.

ejaculation Delivering a sudden rush of semen and sperm through the penis.

embryo A baby that's been developing in the uterus for up to ten weeks.

fallopian tubes The two tubes that join a woman's ovaries to her uterus.

fertilization The fusing together of the genes carried by a sperm and egg.

fetus A baby that's been developing in the uterus for more than ten weeks.

genes A set of instructions in every one of your cells, that helps to determine how you look, think, and develop.

glands Parts of the body that make juices.

hormone A chemical messenger that tells parts of your body when and how to work.

in vitro fertilization Bringing a sperm and egg together in a test tube or dish to conceive a baby artificially.

incubator A special box built to warm a premature baby and give it extra oxygen.

labor The process a mother goes through to squeeze a baby out of her uterus and into the outside world.

marsupials Animals that give birth before their offspring have fully developed. They usually raise their young in a furry pouch.

masturbation To touch your own sexual parts in a way that gives you pleasure.

multiple birth Two or more babies, for example twins or triplets, that develop in a single uterus at the same time.

nipples The parts at the front of a woman's breasts that babies suck on for milk.

nutrients The chemical substances in food that your body needs to survive.

orgasm Ripples of pleasure that people feel when they have sexual intercourse.

ovaries Two small organs, inside a woman's body, that store and release eggs.

oxygen A gas in the air that you breathe. Your body cells need it to work properly.

pelvis The heavy, bowl-shaped set of bones that makes up your bottom and hips.

penis The delivery pipe for a man's urine, semen and sperm.

period Blood and small scraps of tissue that pass out of a woman's body when her uterus lining breaks down each month.

pituitary gland An organ that produces hormones to do with reproduction.

placenta The web of tissue in the uterus that lets nutrients and waste pass between a mother and her developing baby.

pregnant A word describing a woman who has a baby developing in her uterus.

premature The word used to describe a baby that is born before it has spent a full nine months in the uterus.

puberty The time, usually in your early teens, when adolescence starts.

reflex An action that you carry out automatically.

reproduction Creating new life. In humans, this means making babies.

reproductive system In humans, the parts of a man or woman that are used to create a baby and nurture it while it develops.

scrotum The sack on the outside of a man's body that contains his testes.

semen The runny fluid, made by glands at the base of the penis, that carries sperm.

sexual intercourse The joining together of a man and woman, when the man's penis slides inside the woman's vagina.

sperm Swimming cells, made by men, that hold half the genes needed to create a life.

testes Two organs, hanging in the scrotum, that make and store a man's sperm supply.

ultrasound scan An image, produced using high-pitched sound waves, that lets you see a baby developing inside the uterus.

umbilical cord The cord that connects a baby to the placenta in the uterus.

urine The waste liquid, stored in your bladder, that you pass when you urinate.

uterus The sack inside a woman's body that carries and nourishes a developing baby.

vagina The tube that joins a woman's uterus to the outside of her body.

zygote The single cell that's formed when a sperm and egg fuse together.

INDEX